MW01598369

Poetry Society of Texas

An Anthology

of

Student Award Winners 2024

Edited by

Barry Rynk

Editor

Barry Rynk

Aditional Editing

Barbara Blanks

"Painted Pony"

Cover Art by

Toni Andrukaitis

Dedication

To all the students who turn off the electronic devices
long enough to let the creative juices start flowing…

Acknowledgments

Special thanks to PST member Barbara Blanks for her
generous time and expertise in both judging and
editing drafts. Also, thanks to PST members Holly
Jahangiri and Neal Ostman for their unwavering
support throughout the year.

—Barry Rynk, July 2024
PST Chair for Poetry In Schools

Testimonial

On behalf of the Poetry Society of Texas I am honored to recognize the prize-winning student poets for the year 2024. The Society has been publishing this annual anthology since 1989.

I am pleased the Poetry Society of Texas continues the Student Awards Program outreach, and I look forward to the time when winning poets read their poems at the year-end ceremony.

Congratulations to the winners and the teachers who encouraged and motivated these young writers. This book celebrates our young people for reading and writing poetry.

—Rich Weatherly
President of Poetry Society of Texas

From The Chair

I feel fortunate to have been at the helm of this great project for a second year running. My favorite part of being Chair is putting on my editor's cap. I love diving into a stack of student poems—especially poems like the ones in this book—brimming with intelligence, emotion, creativity, and original ideas.

What I've learned from reading these young poets is that life in all its many facets starts young! It's only in the arrogance of old age that youth is conveniently forgotten.

We honor the talented students whose expressions are recorded on these pages, and, undiminished, we honor the teachers and the parents who've done so much to inspire the next-generation of poets.

—Barry Rynk, July 2024
PST Chair of Poetry in Schools

Poetry Society of Texas
The Executive Board 2024

President
Rich Weatherly
N. Richland Hills

Vice-President
Catherine L'Herisson
Garland

Treasurer
Neal Ostman
Colleyville

Recording Secretary
Barbara Blanks
Garland

Corresponding Secretary
Carol Thompson
Tyler

Directors
JDarrell Kirkley
Quitman

Steve Sanders
Fort Worth

Ann Howells
Carrollton

TABLE OF CONTENTS

The ocean

A safe haven
A quiet place
With many sounds
Perfect harmony
Waves
Whales
Birds
A place where ideas thrived
And thoughts wandered
A place with peace
That no human could ever accomplish
Everything worked together for perfection
There were no
Screams
Sirens
Fights
Only music
Made by mother earth herself

Caroline Fleiss

Take my Hand
—"Hand of God" by Michelangelo,
   Sistine Chapel, Vatican City, Italy

Creator, Creation.
I am yours but
You treat me as if
You are mine.

Veins like chords
Near to snap,
You stretch your hand—
And yet mine's slacked.

Out of your clay
I am molded.
Yet the choice to stay
Is one I hold in.

No judgement in your eyes. We sit here bound to die.
This choice fills the space,
So small yet larger than life.
This choice I'll never claim as mine.

And through my disappointments,
And through my flaws,
You continue to offer—
To wash my feet when they're raw.

You are mine.
But you treat me as if
I am yours.
Creation. Creator.

Mischa Rutledge

INSURMOUNTABLE

Wow.
She really said it
and now I wish ...
I don't know what I wish.

It sits between us,
this huge
insurmountable thing.

Like a knife in the middle of the table—
impossible to ignore.
Could be helpful in the right hands, or harmful in the wrong.

Neither one of us wants to pick it up
for fear of what we'll do with it.
We don't want the other to pick it up.
We don't know what they'll do with it either.

I realize
I trust her.
I'll let her do what she will with it.

So she does. She picks it up.
I flinch, expecting her to plunge it into me,
or, worse, herself.
But she doesn't.
She just holds it.

And so
we talk about it,
until the awkwardness is behind us.

I guess
it was surmountable
after all.

Mihika Limaye

FIRE

It dances, confined only by the stone walls holding it back
It is a venomous snake
Beautiful but poised to strike if you come closer
Yet you still want to come closer
As you near
Its warmth washes over you
Bathing you in a hot glow
Just on the edge of painful
Sparks fly out like stars
The flame moves with wind
Its orange and red tongues
Reach out to grab you
You stand back
Watching it reach for empty air
Appreciating the beauty
While scared of the pain

Charlotte Brock-Utne

Winter Wonder

Winter is a winner
In my book

Warm delicious dinner
And a reading nook
Blowing wind outside
Cocoa fireside

Snowflakes on my nose
And socks on my toes
Hallmark is the channel
I'm wearing all flannel

Winter is a winner
In my book

Archer Johnson

Best Friends Forever

Sisterly love is a different kind of love,
A love that shines like the stars above.

A bond that will never be broken,
Our love is a kind unspoken.

The day she was born,
The same day my heart felt warm.

Even though we are three years apart,
She has so much room in my heart.

We used to play with toys and dolls,
Now we go to shopping malls.

When I'm with her, I have no fear,
I never shed a single tear.

Even though we sometimes fight,
We always end up making things right.

It seems like she always smiles,
For her, I would walk one thousand miles.

We will always stick together,
She is my best friend, forever.

Sylvia Schwartz

Grieving Normality

Sometimes we don't notice
The things we could lose
The things we take for granted

It's not until we lose them
That we see
What greatness they were hiding

And the despair you feel
When there is no way you can heal
The wounds that have opened

So you lay in darkness
Wondering how you didn't notice

How the things that were once normal
Are now grieved

It was so easy that you didn't see
How bad it might be
To live without them
Eternally

Jordan Elder

The Sun Drown Place

The sand and the water come by the ton
They stretch for miles all around
I wish I could live there on
That place where sand covers the ground

I watch the dolphins swim past
And the clouds move across the sky
Like a painter moving his brush the opposite of fast
Fish swim past and seagulls fly

I watch the sun set
And as the sun slowly fades, as if it drowned
Like it were caught in a net
And as it becomes a shadow the moon is found

What is this place where the sun drowns
and the water reaches?
Beaches.

Grace Richesin

My Mom
(English sonnet)

My mom is super nice
And is also very kind
She always gives good advice
and has a good mind

She loves to cook
And she likes the color green
She cannot put down a book
And is never ever mean

Her favorite animal is an elephant
And she likes to drink tea
She is very intelligent
And will always agree

This is my mother
She is like no other

Aarush Manikandan

Saint George and The Dragon

Oh how charming he is
As he sits upon his horse
No fear in the world
Of this dragon he has slain

Oh how charming he is
I hope he is soon to be mine
But there's a line before me
Of others calling him divine

Oh how charming he is
The next prince in line
I hope to be his princess
Love of me he might be soon to find

Zeke Franklin

Stereotypes

There are so many things misunderstood,
So many stereotypes that should be gone for good.

Why should all boys have to wear blue?
"Nothing can be pink, not even a shoe."

Why should all girls play with dolls?
"They can't like sports or climbing on walls."

Why are all Jews supposedly cheap?
"They steal your money while you are asleep."

Why are people with EDs just trying to "get attention?"
"They could be eating, without a question."

Why are all Russians alcoholic?
"They are all rude and use no logic."

Why are all blonde girls stupid?
"They all believe in fairytales like Cupid."

Why are all men who are around kids creepy?
"They will probably drug them while they are sleepy."

Why shouldn't men be gay?
'Nobody will want them, they will probably be left astray."

Why can girls cry and boys can't?
"Boys have to be loud, they must chant."

Why are Asians smarter than Americans?
"They are so smart, there is no need for comparison."

There are way too many stereotypes on our Earth,
We have been hearing them since birth.

Sylvia Schwartz

Cost of war

I touch the stone.
The petals of lilies,
Dance in the breeze.

Memories of your face,
Flash as night, day.
Yet the war has changed that face,
And turned it to ash.

The sun's dawn-dappled tree,
Is now gray and withered
Like the hairs on my head.

As a lotus flower blooms,
You rest above,
As you are,
In my heart.

Mary Fisher

Thanksgiving Day

Thanksgiving day is a day for thanks
People are cheery and full of grace
People iron their clothes and shine their shoes
On Thanksgiving Day no one can lose

The kitchen is a hustle and bustle
There are all sorts of foods, even a truffle
The turkey is roasting, they cut the ham
There is even some bread topped off with jam

On top of the table they make an apple pie
Fresh fruits and vegetables from under the sky
Under the table are the cat and dog
Hoping for a treat they have been waiting for so long!

They sit down at the table for the meal they prepared
They prayed to dear lord for all their sins to be spared
They all ate their dinner and there were laughs in the room
And they all stayed over until the glow of the moon

Kate McCullough

The Comeback

The wind-howling Chiefs playing like crazy.
But the Bills are playing lazy.
Then Mahomes throws an interception.
And Allen throws a touchdown.
While Chiefs defenders laying down,
Allen is in the town.
       Mahomes whining.
       Allen is thriving.
       35-34 Kansas City.
       After the game, planning to celebrate in the city.
       But it wasn't to be.
       Because it was he—
       Josh Allen.
Running like a stallion.
Throwing like a goat.
It was one degree but he didn't need a coat.
Last play.
This was quite the day.
Allen drops back.
Bills receivers on the attack.
Allen throws.
Diggs goes.
And ... Bills win!
There is no one quite like him.

Max Singley

The Girl

There she sits. Sitting perfectly still
With a red ribbon on her chest and a feather in her hat.
She has a half-hearted smile and a pain in her eyes,
She had to bite her tongue so she would not cry.
Gone for three years,
Then four,
Then more.
They gave up.
They believed she was gone.
But then they found her.
She was quiet and still
Beside the creek by her house
Where it seemed the cat got the mouse.
The rocks painted red,
Just as red as the ribbon on her chest,
And just as red as the sheets on her bed.
They painted this picture
So she could be there
With a half-hearted smile, and curl in her hair,
And with the ribbon with red right over her heart
Where she had been hurt,
Where the rocks had been painted red.
Just Her, they said, by the creek
In the dirt.
Lying dead.

Ella Vick

Grim

A hooded figure,
Cloaked in black,
Lurks in the shadows,
Tattered and torn,
With a grim smile,
On his face,
And lips sealed shut
Like a tiger
About to pounce
So you can't hear him coming,
Pulling on life's strings,
Until it hits you,
The pain of life's sacrifice,
Kills the soul,
Life slowly slipping away,
Into a puff of black smoke,
Taken by one person,
And his name is
Grim.

Raegan Neuhoff

Winter Chill

The winter chill is here
And I can tell that a snow storm is near
The snow starts to hit the ground
And the grass can no longer be found
I go outside to see the snow
And see its white glow
My hands and feet start to freeze
And then all the sudden I start to feel a really cold breeze
I want to go find some warm air
So I go sit by the fires flare
By the fire I drink, **slurp, slurp, slurp** a cup of warm tea
And the winter chill begins to flee

Layla Napper

The Storm

A peaceful, sweet scent among the pine trees
A sun shining a gray light through a blanket of silver clouds
The swish of small waves crashing against the shore of the lake
Thick air that draws perspiration to your skin
The bugs know

Gusts of air blow through the trees
Leaves flying through the seraphic sunset in the vast sky
Distant rumbling
The only sound you'd hear as the forest quiets
The birds know

An ominous wall of black clouds come rolling in
Livid winds attempt to carry the raindrops into oblivion
Indefatigable hailstones attack anything that is not hidden
The forest knows

A timid white moon peeks through blackened clouds
The bugs begin to sing again, the birds come out
The mushrooms know

Naomi Shellef

Dogs

Paws tucked in
Ready for the night.
Whiskers twitch
Dreams of adventures.
Legs racing at a standstill.
Her head springs up
My reassuring touch.
The moon guides her to me.
She folds herself back to sleep.
Bundles up in the moon's soft blanket.

Serena Elsalameen

Roses of The Rainbow

I can't decide what rose to give.
White and pure, Orange and passion
Peach is modest while Ivory's fashion
Yellow was jealous but now it's for friends
While Blue and Black is for when it ends
Green for health and harmony
Purple for respect and rarity
Red and Lavender mean love
While Pink is for those as sweet as a dove
Dark Lavender's used for regalness
Rainbow roses show happiness
But one rose catches my sight
One that blooms tall and bright
A dark pink rose with twirling vines
With beauty so bright it shines
Thankfulness and honor is what it shows
I knew that this one was the rose.

Emerson Malik

Colors Melting

Pearly whites splash the bronze.
Sienna, tan, and umber shades
are all welcome.

They blend with vivid aquamarine skies.
New drops of fresh pellucid ivory drops
sprinkle down lightly,
as if they were gently tiptoeing into the night,
showering their fresh stories into the earth,
like a gardener watering
her gossamer plants watching them grow.

Yellow bold streaks come in
fizzling with energy,
as if they were fighting their way to be seen.
The glossy meringues sway in, taming the yellow.
They flare out their peaks of sapphire,
like mountains sheering with blue ice and snow.

All the colors bring their own stories to the table.
So, in the end the colors melt,
like sugar over a flame,
like a stove of melting, tropical, fruit juices.
Juicing the stories together.
creates one huge masterpiece.

Natalya Desai

Ripples in the water

There are ripples in the water
That are NOT the blue of the sea,
Nor are they the blue of the sky,
But they are the blue of the ripples in the water
calling out to me.

There are boats on the water
That are NOT the rainbow of the pastel sunset in the evening,
Nor are they the rainbow of my neon paints at home,
But they are the rainbow of the boats on the water
like an array of curves hanging out in the wind and breeze.

There are trees behind the water
That are NOT the green of that velvet dress I wore to tea,
Nor are they the green of the lush summer grass,
But they are the green of the trees behind the water swaying
as if they would soon sway no more.

There are ripples in the water,
With all the boats on top.
Trees are in the background,
Ok, it's time to stop.

Natalia Velasco

Snowflake

A fragile winter butterfly,
Knit by angles in the sky.
If I hold her,
She will weep.
A piece of art
I cannot keep.
Small, descending,
Through the air.
Makes winter's blanket,
White and bare.
One of many butterflies,
Falls with others from the skies.

Kathryn Carter

Snowy Season

The snowflakes make me feel like dancing,
Like prancing,
Like flying,
Like lying,
Down on the couch in front of the fire,
I feel inspired,
to take a walk,
In the freeze,
Snow up to my knees,
Watching the snowflakes blissfully float down,
To the ground,
Without a care,
Swirling in the air,
The unique ice crystals fall onto my face,
I feel like winter is my kind of place,
But when I get cold and go back to my home,
I suddenly lose my desire to roam,
I sit down and sip my chocolaty drink,
Which gives me a lot of time to be quiet and think,
I love snowy winter days, big and small,
But I love going home to blankets most of all.

Bridget Curnes

Chloe

Tail always wagging
Loves to run and play
Always yipping and yapping
Makes me smile every day.

Gentle and friendly
kind and loyal
Always very antsy
Never plain or dull.

Stretches herself out
By the windowsill
Then begins to search about
For something worth a yell.

Loves to joke and play around
Sometimes mischievous too
Loves to play with what she's found
Oh-no it's my new shoe.

Abigail McKee

The Waterfall

Even when the winter comes
When the freeze gives you a scare
Even through the snow and ice
The waterfall's still there

Even when the summer comes
The heat too hot to bear
Even through the sun and sweat
The waterfall's still there

Even when the spring comes
The pollen everywhere
Even through the sneeze and snot
The waterfall's still there

Even when the fall comes
When the trees are dry and bear
Even in the wind and cold
The waterfall's still there
The waterfall's still there

Annelise Reidy

Bumblebees on Flowers

The worker bees that buzz around.
Gathering the molten gold honey

Take it back to the spirally hive.
Where the ceiling stretches high

Only to go out again and find
An ocean of wildflowers.

Amber marigold, ruby red rose,
ocean blue orchids, and sweet-smelling peonies
A shower of beauty, color, and gentleness
Some have ruffled petals and curved leaves.
Others have sharp thorns but fragrant jewels of flowers.

Bumblebees perched near the pollen spouts.
After wandering about
Long, slender tulip pink tongue,
curled into the insides of the flower.
Like taking the treasure from the chest
Short and stout body
Oval and round with stripes
As golden as day
And black as night
Bumblebees on flowers who help give life.

Allison Chu

Coming and Going

The sun's tip rises just above the ocean blue
Like a baby rabbit peeking from the bushes.
It slowly but surely shoots out of the water
Like a baby butterfly beginning to flutter.

The sun is up in the sky, then it sets
Like a pelican shooting down to grab a fish
Then it comes back up and comes again.

It's like my sister going to college.
She leaves to go to school
Then comes back when she has a break.
She always calls and says goodnight.

When the sun goes down
And stars fill the night
It comes back up again
Like my sister coming and going.

Daphne Hoverman

Phone

15% I'm almost dead,
How could this be there's so much to be said.
10% I'm almost out
My life being a phone is such a drought.

5% I'm almost there,
Hey, look my screen has got a tear.
2% so long and goodbye,
The time has come for me to get some shuteye.

Olive Hardy

A Slim And Trim Companion

I am slim and trim like a twig,
But I am quite a handy rig.
I stand tall when I am brand new,
But get short when my end, you chew.

I like to be carried around,
But I do not like getting tossed to the ground.
I give your dreams shape when you doodle,
But don't bend like a soft and supple noodle.

I can turn your imagination into a story,
But never try to take away your glory.
I like when you take me on your travels to France,
But not when you tap me on your desk to make me dance.

I shall be your best friend as long as I live
Sharpen me and I shall give and give.

Maya Bohil

Rain

Falling silently and smoothly
Down it came so beautifully
Almost as though it was an angel
Smelling as wonderfully as flowers after a rain
Feeling calm and relaxed
I breathed in the beautiful smell
It felt so smooth and silky
It could've been lots of angels falling from the sky
Rain is like flower petals
Falling off a flower
Rain is as delicate
As a diamond
So beautiful and small
It falls down from heaven

Lavinia Perkison

Sunrise

A brilliant palate of pink and orange
Paints the sky umber, with the stroke of a brush
Beautiful watercolors start to emerge
But as the colors dry, they leave in a rush
The paint fades to blue, the sky a solid color
Nothing remains of that moment of wonder.

Nina Davies

Just as Human as I am

I forget you are just as human as I am.
Bound by the ticking of times, an unyielding hand,
Yet within this garden, we both tend and till.
For granted I take the cover of your leaves,
Never quite noticing the river of tears that follow thee.

When you sway in the breeze,
I see it as a cathartic release.
Never bothering to think of the energy the wind depletes,
I've only ever thought of you being glee.
Often forgetting, that you're just the same as me.

And when my roots begin to tangle,
I tell you all my tragedies.
You hold me high, working out my knots with time
Too often I forget,
You struggle with just as many roots as I.

And when winter hits and your leaves are forgotten,
Only then do I notice how I've left you unwanted.
To go back in time, to start things off right,
Remember you also seek love, in the shadows, in the shade
To never forget. You are just as human as I am.

Mischa Rutledge

A Red Dancing Floor

Red can be like a rose sitting in my grandmother's
garden, but not this red

Red can be like a ruby ring placed on my mother's
finger, but not this red

Red can be a tragic fire burning down a forest, but
not this red

This red is like a dancing floor, where petals swiftly
twirl shimmy and sway

They dance around a raven black circle

They dance till they fall and then the petals rest
until they can dance round the ring again

Red is like a dancing floor

Rebecca Molina

Hummingbird

Faster, faster.
Wings flap up and down,
so speedy they are
just a blur.

Faster, faster.
The hummingbird dives
through large-branched trees.
Looking for color,
any color.
There is no time
to stop.

Faster, faster.
Flowers—There!
The hummingbird turns
and flies to its meal.
Its beak dips into the yellow flower like a straw.
Sip, hover, sip.
It could sip forever.

Nectar—at last!
It has been ten minutes since its last meal.
Its emerald body gleams in the sunlight.
Its black eyes are focused on the flower
and only the flower.

Faster, faster.
It has been ten minutes since the hummingbird's
last meal. It's off again.
To find more flowers.

Ava Finazzo

Rain

I feel the soft pitter— patter pitter—patter
Standing outside in the rain
My heart jumps and suddenly nothing matters
When I'm out enjoying the day.

Everything I see is covered
In a veil of thick fog
Everything I hear is a mutter
Through the rainy hills in front of us.

The tiny droplets falling down
Felt so refreshing and cool
The puddles of water reflect the brown
Like a mini rain water pool.

I'm so glad
That I went out to play
On this perfect rainy day.

Abigail McKee

Warm Colors

Orange is the color of a campfire,
a family eating Pumpkin Pie,
the color of being wrapped in your mother's arms.

Red is the color of the evening breeze,
a dog curled up in your lap,
the color of waking
to the sounds of rain battering your roof.

Yellow is the color of reading a book,
a ray of sunshine on your face,
the color of being wrapped
in your father's arms.

Brown is the color of taking a walk
in the early morning,
an apple pie being made with your sister beside you,
the color of sitting down after a long day.

White is the color of nothing
and everything,
the color of endings,
a new beginning blossoming within them.

Bridget Curnes

The Kingdom in the River

In the lake where flowers bloom
With the green of ferns and the browns of mushrooms.

Where water lilies dance upon the lake
With pretty tulip pink petals
And a lovely face
Stand proudly in the murky depths with undisguised grace.

Where the lily pads, round and plump as can be
Float on the water for all to see.
A lovely grass green and folded at the edges,
A center of a yellow sheen with gold too.

Where willows bend down to touch the water, so blue.
Where their forest leaves have a kingdom of their own.
A sturdy trunk of penny brown weathered with age.

A kingdom amongst the river
With villagers galore
But one king towers above all
A simple bridge for decor

But his teal is unlike any other
A mother of blue
Like the teal of the ocean too.
In the warm Caribbean dotted with colors,
Like the teal of a beloved dog's collar
Shining with delight
Like the blue of the orchids amid the field
Velvety petals that reach up toward the sun

In this river kingdom
Everything has a place

Allison Chu

Sunflower

The golden petals
As they float down
They sleep quietly
The field bright
With the golden glow
As the sun sets
They shift as if
They were beautiful ballet dancers
Dancing on water
Floating gracefully
With every step
As night falls
The dancers drift
To sleep
For night has come now
And it is time to rest

Riley Stern

Dancing Colors

Twisting and turning
Swaying, dancing
Milky mocha
Dripping on the dirt
Seeping in cracks and roots

Butterfly tutus
Ginger and sage
Flapping wings
Migrating home

Sweeping hair
Flowing ink
Painting a story
With butterfly wings

Pointe shoe pink
Leaping
Pirouette
Graceful as a feather
Paint with no pigment.
Pointe shoe pink

Liv Kane

48

Merry-Go-Round

It spins slowly
It's an awesome ride, watching the world spin around
But something changed
Worry rises and it spins faster
I hook my foot around a bar to stabilize myself
She thinks they're cool
My sweaty hands are desperately gripping onto a handhold
They say my friends are weird and she agrees
The merry-go-round threatens to toss me off
I'm being swung through the air round and round
She's embarrassed of me
And that's it
I let go
Knowing if I get back on,
It will never be the same

Naomi Shellef

Like a Girl

I swim just like a girl you know
and I throw just like one too
I fight just like a girl as well
I am no match for you.

I also run like a girl
That's the way I play
But when they say "like a girl"
I think they mean to say,

That I am the best at doing things
That's how it's gonna be
I'm going to stand right back up
Just you wait and see

Kathryn Carter

Bathtub

Dreams coming true,
You can be a soldier
Or a pilot too!

Play with your bubbles,
Wear Santa's beard.

Don't forget to wash your hair!
You can be a snake,
Or maybe a bear!

Rub-a-dub duckies,
Floating in a line.
A fish swims over,
And a duck yells, MINE!

Scrub-a-dub in the bathtub,
Time to get out and comb your hair

In your mind though,
You're still a bear.

Kathryn Carter

Dandelion

Young, Vibrant that's
What she used to be
Not Yellow though
But beautiful as can be
Out in the fields
Singing her a song.

A group of flowers
Like a family together
Loving each other
One and another
Living in the moment
Out in the world.

Yellow fading into white
The color of snow
So soft and Bright.

One of the family members
Blows away, far away
I can't see it anymore
Just as I can't see my
Great Grandma like I
Could once before.

Her spirit is always here
Curly brown Hair
Knowledge of news and **always**
the perfect audience member
I will remember her.

Young vibrant that's
What she used to be to me.

Eliza Goldfarb

Me!

Change yourself?
Is what they asked
Change yourself.
Is what they said.

But I am me!
Perfectly imperfect me!
Is what I implied
That isn't just a feeling
It's what's in my head.

Inside and out
It's true to see
I'm exactly
Who I want to be.

Change yourself
Is what they replied.
But I said no
Because otherwise
I wouldn't see
Who I want
Me to be.

Lyla Duran

11. JIMMYE INEZ SESSIONS MEMORIAL AWARD —
Honorable Mention

Night Ocean

In the ocean,
oxford blue mountains of water
clap together,
and shatter into pieces with memories,
pulled down into the forgotten depths of the sea.

Piper Flanagan

Rainstorm

Gray clouds fill the sky
When the clouds get too full they cry
Little droplets of water pitter-patter on the sidewalk
Stick out your tongue, you'll taste the story each one tells
Booms of thunder sing a song about where they're going
The wind softly whispers to the sky "oh why, oh why"
The wonders of nature no one knows
But if you pay close attention then you too will grow.

Lily Azul Whitfield

Blankets

I long for words like soft blankets,
To offer solace in moments of sorrow or anger.
Hoping to dull my daggered words.
I yearn for speech that soothes like gentle whispers,
And vowels to flow like honey, not poison.

I yearn to be a harbor after weary days.
A place for taxed travelers to rest in peace.
Yet too often my words wound,
hurting those I hold dear.
Always the devil that offers sorrow rather than care.

Perhaps someday, I'll master the art of care,
balancing the scale of support and cheer.
But until then, I'll wrangle my words,
mindful of their hidden harm.
Though my heart may strain, in silence, I'll find peaceful arms.

Mischa Rutledge

Gone.

Lost in the woods
without a map
Existing in a solar system
with no sun
guideless
lightless
hopeless
They say home is where the heart is
but how do you know your heart
when its teachers are
gone.
gone.
gone.
So there you are
wandering aimlessly in a cold, dark, empty,
parentless
void
Seeking some light, some warmth,
some love
to lead you home
Though some part of you knows it will always be here
this pain, this emptiness,
this empty space in the puzzle that is you,
the piece the universe stole
before you knew what it meant
before you could see them, know them, love them
the way they deserved.
Gone.

Caroline Hayes

15. karla k. morton Award — First Place

Melting away

Summer hits you like a double decker bus,
sending you sprawling over the curb of Spring
and hauling you up by the scruff of your shirt.

It stops to let you pick wet gravel out of your eyes
before it presses your face against the window of the past,
breath-fogged glass freezing as Summer cries There!
the grainy ribbon-reel unfurls outside and suddenly

There! is the ice cream truck, lurid letters faded by sun,
There! is the wet grass muddying the bathroom tiles,
There! is the rain so warm you could have showered in it,
There! is the gravel that scraped your feet till they bled

as you gulped the downpour like lemonade and laughed wildly
and danced like fire was burning red-hot beneath your feet.
Time blurs behind whipping strands of rain-slick hair,
and the years that melted away smudge together,
sticky memories dripping through your clenched fists
like sugared popsicles,

which the dogs licked up while you cried,
dirt stinging in the old cuts on your feet.
And now you are older and the rain lashes the windows
until they rattle blue-lipped in their frames

and the dogs are scratching at your door,
whimpering, begging you to let them come in
and lick up the blood.

Carolyn Mitchell

A Lonesome Twinkle

In the endless roam of the midnight sky,
Millions of Stars glisten, distant yet close by,
Each one so stunning, a blinding light,
Yet in their splendor, a curious plight.

Alone they burn, in cosmic ballet.
A lonesome path, each night after day.
A breathtaking sight, they twinkle alone,
In a universe vast, they make their presence known.

But do they ever yearn,
For the warmth of another, amidst endless years,
Though millions of them, are apart,
A lonely existence in the cosmos' grandeur.

Yet in their solitude, they find their grace.
A silent witness to the vastness untold.
For even in loneliness, they shimmer bright,
A testament to resilience, in the cosmic night.

Here we sit glazed in awe,
For in their solitude, they find their flaw.
A single star may shine, but together they gleam.
In the vastness of night, an endless dream.

Mischa Rutledge

Tempest

I once knew a girl
Who drank moonlight and bathed in stardust
I saw her dance through the moss-covered trees
Her skirt flowing freely around her
I saw her laugh with the sun
And sing with the rain
I saw her lay by the stream
Wondering up at the sky.

I lost this girl that I knew
Behind a desk
Her hands folded neatly,
Her wild, fiery curls tucked away
She disappeared, gone to
Thick textbooks and long essays.

I see her again from time to time
In a scarlet golden sunset
In a field of wildflowers
In the reflection of a deep, beautiful blue sea
But she's never here long.

I guess that's how she'd want it,
Coming and going, roaming free
Like a light breeze
Or an untamed tempest.

Caroline Hayes

Friendship

Close enough to be family
Far enough to not always annoy me
There to brighten my day
There to make me smile
Shared many laughs
Shared many cries
Cheered me up
Brought me down
Hugged me
Yelled at me
Showed me when I was wrong
But still loved when I was rude
Taught me many things

Caroline Fleiss

16. GENEVA M. FULGHAM AWARD

(No entries)

Comfort Food

Standing on my tiptoes, learning to chop
The sharp scent of cilantro mixed with buttery onions
Wafting over my head.
Years later, having my fifth bowl of the week,
The crisp celery lifting the tender chicken
As my friend and I giggle over the phone
Warming away almost all the sickness.
I'm older now, tossing a handful of scarlet carrots
Into the pot of aromatic broth and dancing pasta
Enjoying a bowl of my own creation
With a crunchy slice of perfectly toasted bread
And the people I love most.

Caroline Hayes

17. "My Favorite Soup Reminds Me" AWARD — Second Place

Nonna's ingredient

The bowl warmed my hands
Excited my mouth
Not too cold
Not too hot
Perfect
Déjà vu
My Nonna worked hard
She made it so everyone would be happy
With her secret ingredient:
Love
And three kisses

Caroline Fleiss

APPENDIX: Winning Roster and Student/Teacher Information

#1. MAHAN PRIZE (Grades 8–12)
Offered and Judged by Budd Powell Mahan

1st. "The ocean" by Caroline Fleiss
8th grade, The Hockaday School
11600 Welch Rd.
Dallas, TX 75229
Dr. Lauren Miskin

2nd. "Take my Hand" by Mischa Rutledge
10th grade, The Hockaday School
11600 Welch Rd.
Dallas, TX 75229
Mrs. Sara Harder

(No 3rd - HM)

#2. BEATRICE M. LAND MEMORIAL CONTEST (Grades 6–7)

Offered and Judged by Catherine L'Herisson

1st. "INSURMOUNTABLE" by Mihika Limaye
7th grade, Canyon Vista Middle School
8455 Spicewood Springs Rd.
Austin, TX 78759
Ms. Jessica Harper

2nd. "FIRE" by Charlotte Brock-Utne
6th grade, Good Shepherd Episcopal School
11110 Midway Rd.
Dallas, TX 75229
Ms. Kim Campbell

3rd. "Winter Wonder" by Archer Johnson
6th grade, Good Shepherd Episcopal School
11110 Midway Rd.
Dallas, TX 75244
Ms. Kim Campbell

HM. "Best Friends Forever" by Sylvia Schwartz
7th grade, Levine Academy
18011 Hillcrest Rd.
Dallas, TX 75252
Ms. Joanie Geffen

HM. "Grieving Normality" by Jordan Elder
6th grade, Good Shepherd Episcopal School
11110 Midway Rd.
Dallas, TX 75229
Ms. Kim Campbell

#3. NAOMI STROUD SIMMONS MEMORIAL AWARD
(Grades 6–7)
Offered by the family of Naomi Stroud Simmons
Judged by Richard Kushmaul

1st. "The Sun Drown Place" by Grace Richesin
6th grade, Good Shepherd Episcopal School
11110 Midway Rd.
Dallas, TX 75229
Ms. Kim Campbell

2nd. "My Mom" by Aarush Manikandan
6th grade, Good Shepherd Episcopal School
11110 Midway Rd.
Dallas, TX 75229
Ms. Kim Campbell

3rd. "Saint George and The Dragon" by Zeke Franklin
6th grade, Good Shepherd Episcopal School
11110 Midway Rd.
Dallas, TX 75229
Ms. Kim Campbell

HM. "Stereotypes" by Sylvia Schwartz
7th grade, Levine Academy
18011 Hillcrest Rd.
Dallas, TX 75252
Ms. Joanie Geffen

#4. KARLE WILSON BAKER MEMORIAL PRIZE (Grades 6–7)
Offered and Judged by Patrick Lee Marshall

1st. "Cost of war" by Mary Fisher
7th grade, Daggett Montessori
801 W. Jessamine St.
Ft. Worth, TX 76110
Ms. Jennifer Whitman

2nd. "Thanksgiving Day" by Kate McCullough
6th grade, Good Shepherd Episcopal School
11110 Midway Road
Dallas, TX 75229
Ms. Kim Campbell

3rd. "The Comeback" by Max Singley
6th grade, Good Shepherd Episcopal School
11110 Midway Rd.
Dallas, TX 75229
Ms. Kim Campbell

HM. "The Girl" by Ella Vick
6th grade, Good Shepherd Episcopal School
11110 Midway Rd.
Dallas, TX 75229
Ms. Kim Campbell

HM. "Grim" by Raegan Neuhoff
6th grade, Good Shepherd Episcopal School
11110 Midway Rd.
Dallas, TX 75229
Ms. Kim Campbell

HM. "Winter Chill" by Layla Napper
6th grade, Good Shepherd Episcopal School
11110 Midway Rd.
Dallas, TX 75229
Ms. Kim Campbell

#5. MONTGOMERY AWARD (Grades 4–5)
Established in the will of Estelle Stewart to honor Whitney and Vaida
Montgomery, Thelma Evelyn Boyd, and Genevieve Boyd Stewart
Judged by Cindy Wood

1st. "The Storm" by Naomi Shellef
5th grade, The Hockaday School
11600 Welch Rd.
Dallas, TX 75229
Ms. Deidre Thomson

2nd. "Dogs" by Serena Elsalameen
5th grade, The Hockaday School
11600 Welch Rd.
Dallas, Texas 75229
Mrs. Lisa Waugh

3rd. "Roses of The Rainbow" by Emerson Malik
5th grade, The Hockaday School
11600 Welch Rd.
Dallas, TX 75229
Mrs. Lisa Waugh

HM. "Colors Melting" by Natalya Desai
5th grade, The Hockaday School
11600 Welch Rd.
Dallas, TX 75229
Mrs. Lisa Waugh

HM. "Ripples in the Water" by Natalia Velasco
5th grade, The Hockaday School
11600 Welch Rd.
Dallas, TX 75229
Mrs. Lisa Waugh

#6. MILDRED VORPAHL BAASS MEMORIAL AWARD
(Grades 4–5)
Offered and Judged by Nancy Baass

1st. "Snowflake" by Kathryn Carter
5th grade, The Hockaday School
11600 Welch Rd.
Dallas, TX 75229
Mrs. Lisa Waugh

2nd. "Snowy Season" by Bridget Curnes
5th grade, The Hockaday School
11600 Welch Rd.
Dallas, TX 75229
Mrs. Lisa Waugh

3rd. "Chloe" by Abigail McKee
5th grade, The Hockaday School
11600 Welch Rd.
Dallas, TX 75229
Mrs. Lisa Waugh

HM. "The Waterfall" by Annelise Reidy
5th grade, The Hockaday School
11600 Welch Rd.
Dallas, TX 75229
Ms. Deidre Thomson

#7. JOHN D. VAUGHN MEMORIAL AWARD (Grades 4– 5)
Offered by Aman Khan
Judged by Barbara Blanks

1st. "Bumblebees on Flowers" by Allison Chu
5th grade, The Hockaday School
11600 Welch Rd.
Dallas, TX 75229
Mrs. Lisa Waugh

2nd. "Coming and Going" by Daphne Hoverman
5th grade, The Hockaday School
11600 Welch Rd.
Dallas, TX 75229
Mrs. Lisa Waugh

3rd. "Phone" by Olive Hardy
5th grade, The Hockaday School
11600 Welch Rd.
Dallas, TX 75229
Mrs. Lisa Waugh

HM. "A Slim And Trim Companion" by Maya Bohil
5th grade, The Hockaday school
11600 Welch Rd.
Dallas TX 75229
Ms. Deidre Thomson

HM. "Rain" by Lavinia Perkison
5th grade, The Hockaday School
11600 Welch Rd.
Dallas, TX 75229
Mrs. Lisa Waugh

HM. "Sunrise" by Nina Davies
5th grade, The Hockaday School
11600 Welch Rd.
Dallas, TX 75229
Mrs. Lisa Waugh

#8. VIOLETTE NEWTON MEMORIAL AWARD (Grades 9– 12)
Offered by Poets Northwest
Judged by Eric Blanchard

1st. "Just as Human as I am" by Mischa Rutledge
10th grade, The Hockaday School
11600 Welch Rd.
Dallas, TX 75229
Mrs. Sara Harder

(No 2nd - HM)

#9. MARCELLA SIEGEL CONTEST (Grade 5)
Offered and judged by Ann Howells

1st. "A Red Dancing Floor" by Rebecca Molina
5th grade, The Hockaday School
11600 Welch Rd.
Dallas, TX 75229
Mrs. Lisa Waugh

2nd. "Hummingbird" by Ava Finazzo
5th grade, The Hockaday School
11600 Welch Rd.
Dallas, TX 75229
Mrs. Lisa Waugh

3rd. "Rain" by Abigail McKee
5th grade, The Hockaday School
11600 Welch Rd.
Dallas, TX 75229
Mrs. Lisa Waugh

HM. "Warm Colors" by Bridget Curnes
5th grade, The Hockaday School
11600 Welch Rd.
Dallas, TX 75229
Mrs. Lisa Waugh

#10. MILLER MEMORIAL CONTEST (Grades 3– 5)
Offered and Judged by Terry J. Miller

1st. "The Kingdom in the River" by Allison Chu
5th grade, The Hockaday School
11600 Welch Rd.
Dallas, TX 75229
Mrs. Lisa Waugh

2nd. "Sunflower" by Riley Stern
5th grade, The Hockaday School
11600 Welch Rd.
Dallas, TX 75229
Ms. Deidre Thomson

3rd. "Dancing Colors" by Liv Kane
5th grade, The Hockaday School
11600 Welch Rd.
Dallas, TX 75229
Mrs. Lisa Waugh

HM. "Merry-Go-Round" by Naomi Shellef
5th grade, The Hockaday School
11600 Welch Rd.
Dallas, TX 75229
Ms. Deidre Thomson

HM. "Like a Girl" by Kathryn Carter
5th grade, The Hockaday School
11600 Welch Rd.
Dallas, TX 75229
Mrs. Lisa Waugh

#11. JIMMYE INEZ SESSIONS MEMORIAL AWARD (Grades 4–5)

Offered and Judged by Laurie Kolp

1st. "Bathtub" by Kathryn Carter
5th grade, The Hockaday School
11600 Welch Rd.
Dallas, TX 75229
Mrs. Lisa Waugh

2nd. "Dandelion" by Eliza Goldfarb
5th grade, The Hockaday School
11600 Welch Rd.
Dallas, TX 75229
Mrs. Lisa Waugh

3rd. "Me!" by Lyla Duran
5th grade, The Hockaday School
11600 Welch Road
Dallas, TX 75229
Ms. Lisa Waugh

HM. "Night Ocean" by Piper Flanagan
5th grade, The Hockaday School
11600 Welch Rd.
Dallas, TX 75229
Mrs. Lisa Waugh

HM. "Rainstorm" by Lily Azul Whitfield
5th grade, The Hockaday School
11600 Welch Rd.
Dallas, TX 75229
Mrs. Lisa Waugh

#12. JAMES PAUL HOLCOMB MEMORIAL PRIZE (Grades 9–12)
Offered and judged by L. L. Lee

1st. "Blankets" by Mischa Rutledge
10th grade, The Hockaday School
11600 Welch Rd.
Dallas, TX 75229
Mrs. Sarah Harder

(No 2nd - HM)

#13. THE HONORES PRIZE (Grades 8– 12)
Offered and judged by Nancy De Honores

1st. "Gone" by Caroline Hayes
8th grade, The Hockaday School
11600 Welch Rd.
Dallas, TX 75229
Dr. Lauren Miskin

(No 2nd - HM)

#14. karla k. morton Award (Grades 9– 12)
Offered and judged by karla k. morton

1st. "Melting Away" by Caroline Mitchell
9th grade, The Hockaday School
11600 Welch Rd.
Dallas, TX 75229
Ms. Melissa Allan

2nd. "A Lonesome Twinkle" by Mischa Rutledge
10th grade, The Hockaday School
11600 Welch Rd.
Dallas, TX 75229
Mrs. Sara Harder

(No 3rd - HM)

#15. DIANE GLANCY AWARD (Grades 8– 9)
Offered and Judged by Diane Glancy

1st. "Tempest" by Caroline Hayes
8th grade, The Hockaday School
11600 Welch Rd.
Dallas, TX 75229
Dr. Lauren Miskin

2nd. "Friendship" by Caroline Fleiss
8th grade, The Hockaday School
11600 Welch Rd.
Dallas, TX 75229
Dr. Lauren Miskin

(No 3rd - HM)

#16. GENEVA M. FULGHAM AWARD (Grades 10– 12)
Sponsored by Geneva M. Fulgham
Judged by Neal Ostman

No entries

#17. "MY FAVORITE SOUP REMINDS ME" AWARD (Grades 7–9)

Offered and Judged by Carol Thompson

1st. "Comfort Food" by Caroline Hayes
8th grade, The Hockaday School
11600 Welch Rd.
Dallas, TX 75229
Dr. Lauren Miskin

2nd. "Nonna's ingredient" by Caroline Fleiss
8th grade, The Hockaday School
11600 Welch Rd.
Dallas, TX 75229
Dr. Lauren Miskin

Made in the USA
Columbia, SC
19 August 2024

40228297R10046